Grammar Reference for Test Takers:

A Comprehensive Grammar Guide for Individuals Preparing for Standardized Tests Such as TOEFL, IELTS, or SAT

By

Melanie P. Salter

CLASSES OF CONJUNCTIONS. [Footnote: For classified lists, see pp. 190,191.]

+Hints for Oral Instruction+.—*Frogs, antelopes, and kangaroos can jump.* Here the three nouns are of the same rank in the sentence. All are subjects of *can jump. War has ceased, and peace has come.* In this compound sentence, there are two clauses of the same rank. The word *and* connects the subjects of *can jump,* in the first sentence: and the two clauses, in the second. All words that connect words, phrases, or clauses of the *same rank* are called +Co-ordinate Conjunctions+.

If you have tears, prepare to shed them now. I will go, because you need me. Here *if* joins the clause, *you have tears*, as a modifier, expressing condition, to the independent clause, *prepare to shed them now;* and *because* connects *you need me*, as a modifier, expressing reason or cause, to the independent clause, *I will go.* These and all such conjunctions as connect dependent clauses to clauses of a *higher rank* are called +Subordinate Conjunctions+.

Let the teacher illustrate the meaning and use of the words *subordinate* and *co-ordinate*.

DEFINITIONS.

+*Co-ordinate Conjunctions* are such as connect words, phrases, or clauses of the same rank+.

+*Subordinate Conjunctions* are such as connect clauses of different rank+.

SENTENCE-BUILDING.

Build four short sentences for each of the three *co-ordinate conjunctions* that follow. In the first, let the conjunction be used to connect principal parts of a sentence; in the second, to connect word modifiers; in the third, to connect phrase modifiers; and in the fourth, to connect independent clauses.

And, or, but.

Write four short complex sentences containing the four *subordinate conjunctions* that follow. Let the first be used to introduce a noun clause, and the other three to connect adverb clauses to independent clauses.

That, for, if, because.

CLASSES OF CONJUNCTIONS. [Footnote: For classified lists, see pp. 190,191.]

+Hints for Oral Instruction+.—*Frogs, antelopes, and kangaroos can jump.* Here the three nouns are of the same rank in the sentence. All are subjects of *can jump*. *War has ceased, and peace has come.* In this compound sentence, there are two clauses of the same rank. The word *and* connects the subjects of *can jump*, in the first sentence: and the two clauses, in the second. All words that connect words, phrases, or clauses of the *same rank* are called +Co-ordinate Conjunctions+.

If you have tears, prepare to shed them now. I will go, because you need me. Here *if* joins the clause, *you have tears*, as a modifier, expressing condition, to the independent clause, *prepare to shed them now;* and *because* connects *you need me*, as a modifier, expressing reason or cause, to the independent clause, *I will go.* These and all such conjunctions as connect dependent clauses to clauses of a *higher rank* are called +Subordinate Conjunctions+.

Let the teacher illustrate the meaning and use of the words *subordinate* and *co-ordinate*.

DEFINITIONS.

+*Co-ordinate Conjunctions* are such as connect words, phrases, or clauses of the same rank+.

+*Subordinate Conjunctions* are such as connect clauses of different rank+.

SENTENCE-BUILDING.

Build four short sentences for each of the three *co-ordinate conjunctions* that follow. In the first, let the conjunction be used to connect principal parts of a sentence; in the second, to connect word modifiers; in the third, to connect phrase modifiers; and in the fourth, to connect independent clauses.

And, or, but.

Write four short complex sentences containing the four *subordinate conjunctions* that follow. Let the first be used to introduce a noun clause, and the other three to connect adverb clauses to independent clauses.

That, for, if, because.

REVIEW QUESTIONS.

What new subject begins with page 95? Name and define the different classes of nouns. Illustrate by examples the difference between common nouns and proper nouns. Name and define the different classes of pronouns. Can the pronoun *I* be used to stand for the one spoken to?—the one spoken of? Does the relative pronoun distinguish by its *form* the speaker, the one spoken to, and the one spoken of? Illustrate. Can any other class of pronouns be used to connect clauses?

For what do interrogative pronouns stand? Illustrate. Where may the antecedent of an interrogative pronoun generally be found? *Ans.—The antecedent of an interrogative pronoun may generally lie found in the answer to the question.*

Name and define the different classes of adjectives. Give an example of each class. Name and define the different classes of verbs, made with respect to their meaning. Give an example of each class. Name and define the different classes of verbs, made with respect to their form. Give an example of each class.

Name and define the different classes of adverbs. Give examples of each kind. Name and define the different classes of conjunctions. Illustrate by examples.

Are prepositions and interjections subdivided? (See "Schemes" for the conjunction, the preposition, and the interjection, p. 188.)

+To the Teacher+.—See COMPOSITION EXERCISES in the Supplement— Selection from Dr. John Brown.

We suggest that other selections from literature be made and these exercises continued.

MODIFICATIONS OF THE PARTS OF SPEECH.

NOUNS AND PRONOUNS.

You have learned that two words may express a thought, and that the thought may be varied by adding modifying words. You are now to learn that the meaning or use of a word may sometimes be changed by simply changing its *form*. The English language has lost many of its inflections, or forms, so that frequently changes in the meaning and use of words are not marked by changes in form. These *changes* in the *form*, *meaning*, and *use* of the parts of speech, we call their +Modifications+.

The boy shouts. The boys shout. I have changed the form of the subject *boy* by adding an *s* to it. The meaning has changed. *Boy* denotes *one* lad; *boys*, *two or more* lads. This change in the form and meaning of nouns is called +Number+. The word *boy*, denoting one thing, is in the +Singular Number;+ and *boys*, denoting more than one thing, is in the +Plural Number+.

Let the teacher write other nouns on the board, and require the pupils to form the plural of them.

DEFINITIONS.

+*Modifications of the Parts of Speech* are changes in their form, meaning, and use+.

NUMBER.

+*Number* is that modification of a noun or pronoun which denotes one thing or more than one+.

+The *Singular Number* denotes one thing+.

+The *Plural Number* denotes more than one thing+.

+RULE.—The *plural* of nouns is regularly formed by adding *s* to the singular+.

Write the plural of the following nouns.

Tree, bird, insect, cricket, grasshopper, wing, stick, stone, flower, meadow, pasture, grove, worm, bug, cow, eagle, hawk, wren, plough, shovel.

When a singular noun ends in the sound of *s, x, z, sh,* or *ch,* it is not easy to add the sound of *s,* so *es* is added to make another syllable.

Write the plural of the following nouns.

Guess, box, topaz, lash, birch, compass, fox, waltz, sash, bench, gas, tax, adz, brush, arch.

Many nouns ending in *o* preceded by a consonant form the plural by adding *es* without increasing the number of syllables.

Write the plural of the following nouns.

Hero, cargo, negro, potato, echo, volcano, mosquito, motto.

Common nouns ending in *y* preceded by a consonant form the plural by changing *y* into *i* and adding *es* without increasing the number of syllables.

Write the plural of the following nouns.

Lady, balcony, family, city, country, daisy, fairy, cherry, study, sky.

Some nouns ending in *f* and *fe* form the plural by changing *f* or *fe* into *ves* without increasing the number of syllables.

Write the plural of the following nouns.

Sheaf, loaf, beef, thief, calf, half, elf, shelf, self, wolf, life, knife, wife.

NUMBER.

From the following list of nouns, select, and write in separate columns: 1st. Those that have no plural; 2d. Those that have no singular; 3d. Those that are alike in both numbers.

Pride, wages, trousers, cider, suds, victuals, milk, riches, flax, courage, sheep, deer, flour, idleness, tidings, thanks, ashes, scissors, swine, heathen.

The following nouns have very irregular plurals. Learn to spell the plurals.

Singular. Plural. Singular. Plural.
Man, men. Foot, feet.
Woman, women. Ox, oxen.
Child, children. Tooth, teeth.
Mouse, mice. Goose, geese.

Learn the following plurals and compare them with the groups in the preceding Lesson.

Moneys, flies, chimneys, valleys, stories, berries, lilies, turkeys, monkeys, cuckoos, pianos, vetoes, solos, folios, gulfs, chiefs, leaves, roofs, scarfs, inches.

NOUNS AND PRONOUNS.—GENDER.

+Hints for Oral Instruction+.—*The lion was caged. The lioness was caged*. In the first sentence, something was said about a *male* lion; and in the second, something was said about a *female* lion. Modifications of the noun to denote the sex of the object, we call +Gender+. Knowing the sex of the object, you know the gender of its name. The word *lion*, denoting a male animal, is in the +Masculine Gender;+ and *lioness*, denoting a female lion, is in the +Feminine Gender+.

The names of things *without* sex are in the +Neuter Gender+.

Such words as *cousin, child, friend, neighbor,* may be *either masculine or feminine*.

+DEFINITIONS.

Gender is that modification of a noun or pronoun which denotes sex.

The *Masculine Gender* denotes the male sex.

The *Feminine Gender* denotes the female sex.

The *Neuter Gender* denotes want of sex+.

The masculine is distinguished from the feminine in three ways:—

1st. By a difference in the ending of the nouns.

2d. By different words in the compound names.

3d. By words wholly or radically different.

Arrange the following pairs in separate columns with reference to these ways.

Abbot, abbess; actor, actress; Francis, Frances; Jesse, Jessie; bachelor, maid; beau, belle; monk, nun; gander, goose; administrator, administratrix; baron, baroness; count, countess; czar, czarina; don, donna; boy, girl; drake, duck; lord, lady; nephew, niece; landlord, landlady; gentleman, gentlewoman; peacock, peahen; duke, duchess; hero, heroine; host, hostess; Jew, Jewess; man-servant, maid-servant; sir, madam; wizard, witch; marquis, marchioness; widow, widower; heir, heiress; Paul, Pauline; Augustus, Augusta.

REVIEW QUESTIONS.

What new way of varying the meaning of words is introduced in Lesson 78? Illustrate. What are modifications of the parts of speech? What is number? How many numbers are there? Name and define each. Give the rule for forming the plural of nouns. Illustrate the variations of this rule. What is gender? How many genders are there? Name and define each. In how many ways are the genders distinguished? Illustrate.

NOUNS AND PRONOUNS.—PERSON AND CASE.

+Hints for Oral Instruction+.—*Number* and *gender*, as you have already learned, are modifications affecting the *meaning* of nouns and pronouns. Number is almost always indicated by the ending; gender, sometimes. There are two other modifications which refer not to changes in the *meaning* of nouns and pronouns, but to their different *uses* and *relations*. In the English language, these changes are not often indicated by a change of *form*.

I Paul have written. *Paul, thou* art beside thyself. *He* brought *Paul* before Agrippa. In these three sentences the word *Paul* has *three different uses*. In the first, it is used as the name of the *speaker*; in the second, as the name of *one spoken to*; in the third, as the name of *one spoken of*. You will notice that the *form* of the noun was not changed. This change in the use of nouns and pronouns is called +Person+. The word *I* in the first sentence, the word *thou* in the second, and the word *he* in the third have each a different use. *I, thou,* and *he* are personal pronouns, and, as you have learned, distinguish *person* by their *form*. *I,* denoting the speaker, is in the +First Person+; *thou,* denoting the one spoken to, is in the +Second Person+; and *he,* denoting the one spoken of, is in the +Third Person+.

Personal pronouns and *verbs* are the only words that distinguish person by their form.

The bear killed the man. The man killed the bear. The bear's grease was made into hair oil. In the first sentence, the bear is represented as *performing* an action; in the second, as *receiving* an action; in the third, as *possessing* something. So the word *bear* in these sentences has three different uses. These uses of nouns are called +Cases+. The use of a noun as subject is called the +Nominative Case+; its use as object is called the +Objective Case+; and its use to denote possession is called the +Possessive Case+.

The *possessive* is the only case of nouns that is indicated by a change in *form*.

A noun or pronoun used as an *attribute* complement is in the *nominative case*. A noun or pronoun following a preposition as the principal word of a phrase is in the *objective case*. *I* and *he* are *nominative* forms. *Me* and *him* are *objective* forms.

The following sentences are therefore incorrect: It is *me*; It is *him*; *Me* gave the pen to *he*.

+DEFINITIONS.+

Person is that modification of a noun or pronoun which denotes the speaker, the one spoken to, or the one spoken of.

The *First Person* denotes the one speaking.

The *Second Person* denotes the one spoken to.

The *Third Person* denotes the one spoken of.

Case is that modification of a noun or pronoun which denotes its office in the sentence.

The *Nominative Case of a noun or pronoun* denotes its office as subject or as attribute complement.

The *Possessive Case of a noun or pronoun* denotes its office as possessive modifier.

The *Objective Case of a noun or pronoun* denotes its office as object complement, or as principal word in a prepositional phrase+.

NOUNS AND PRONOUNS.—PERSON AND CASE.

Tell the *person* and *case* of each of the following nouns and pronouns.

+Remember+ that a noun or pronoun used as an *explanatory modifier* is in the same case as the word which it explains, and that a noun or pronoun used *independently* is in the *nominative case*.

We Americans do things in a hurry.
You Englishmen take more time to think.
The Germans do their work with the most patience and deliberation.
We boys desire a holiday.
Come on, my men; I will lead you.
I, your teacher, desire your success.
You, my pupils, are attentive.
I called on Tom, the tinker.
Friends, countrymen, and lovers, hear me for my cause.

Write simple sentences in which each of the following nouns shall be used in the *three persons* and in the *three cases*.

Andrew Jackson, Alexander, Yankees.

Write a sentence containing a noun in the *nominative* case, used as an *attribute;* one in the *nominative,* used as an *explanatory modifier;* one in the *nominative,* used independently.

Write a sentence containing a noun in the *objective case,* used to *complete two predicate verbs*; one used to *complete* a *participle*; one used to *complete* an *infinitive*; one used *with a preposition* to make a phrase; one used as an *explanatory modifier*.

+To the Teacher+.—See pp. 183, 184.

NOUNS AND PRONOUNS.—DECLENSION.

+DEFINITION.—*Declension* is the arrangement of the cases of nouns and pronouns in the two numbers+.

Declension of Nouns.

LADY.

Singular. Plural. Nom. lady, ladies, *Pos.* lady's, ladies', *Obj.* lady; ladies.

CHILD.

Singular. Plural. Nom. child, children, *Pos.* child's, children's, *Obj.* child; children.

Declension of Pronouns.

PERSONAL PRONOUNS.

FIRST PERSON.

Singular. Plural. Nom. I, we, *Pos.* my *or* mine, our *or* ours, *Obj.* me; us.

SECOND PERSON—*common form.*

Singular. Plural. Nom. you, you, *Pos.* your *or* yours, your *or* yours, *Obj.* you; you.

SECOND PERSON—*old form.*

Singular. Plural. Nom. thou, ye or you, *Pos.* thy *or* thine, your *or* yours, *Obj.* thee; you.

THIRD PERSON—*masculine.*

Singular. Plural. Nom. he, they, *Pos.* his, their *or* theirs, *Obj.* him; them.

THIRD PERSON—*feminine.*

Singular. Plural. Nom. she, they, *Pos.* her *or* hers, their *or* theirs, *Obj.* her; them.

THIRD PERSON——*neuter.*

Singular. Plural. Nom. it, they, *Pos.* its, their *or* theirs, *Obj.* it; them.

Mine, ours, yours, thine, hers, and *theirs* are used when the name of the thing possessed is omitted; as, This rose is *yours* = This rose is *your rose.*

COMPOUND PERSONAL PRONOUNS.

By joining the word *self* to the possessive forms *my, thy, your,* and to the objective forms *him, her, it,* the +Compound Personal Pronouns+ are formed. They have no possessive case, and are alike in the nominative and the objective.

Their plurals are *ourselves, yourselves,* and *themselves.* Form the *compound personal pronouns,* and write their declension.

RELATIVE AND INTERROGATIVE PRONOUNS.

Sing. and Plu. Nom. who, *Pos.* whose, *Obj.* whom.

Sing. and Plu. Nom. which, *Pos.* whose, *Obj.* which.

Of which is often used instead of the possessive form of the latter pronoun.

Sing. and Plu. Nom. that, *Pos.* ——, *Obj.* that.

Sing. and Plu. Nom. what, *Pos.* ——, *Obj.* what.

Ever and *soever* are added to *who, which,* and *what* to form the +Compound Relative Pronouns+. They are used when the antecedent is omitted. For declension, see above.

POSSESSIVE FORMS.

+RULE.—The *possessive case* of nouns is formed in the singular by adding to the nominative the apostrophe and the letter *s* ('s); in the plural, by adding (') only. If the plural does not end in *s*, the apostrophe and the *s* are both added+.

Write the *possessive singular* and the *possessive plural* of the following nouns, and place an appropriate noun after each.

Robin, friend, fly, hero, woman, bee, mouse, cuckoo, fox, ox, man, thief,
fairy, mosquito, wolf, shepherd, farmer, child, neighbor, cow.

Possession may be expressed also by the preposition *of* and the *objective*; as, the *mosquito's* bill = the bill *of* the *mosquito*.

The possessive sign ('s) is confined *chiefly* to the names of persons and animals.

We do not say the *chair's* legs, but the legs *of* the *chair*. Regard must be had also to the *sound*.

IMPROVE THE FOLLOWING EXPRESSIONS, and expand each into a simple sentence.

The sky's color; the cloud's brilliancy; the rose's leaves; my uncle's partner's house; George's father's friend's farm; the mane of the horse of my brother; my brother's horse's mane.

When there are several possessive nouns, all belonging to one word, the possessive sign is added to the last only. If they modify different words, the sign is added to each.

CORRECT THE FOLLOWING EXPRESSIONS, and expand each into a simple sentence.

+Model+.—*Webster and Worcester's dictionary may be bought at Ticknor's and Field's book-store.*

The possessive sign should be added to *Webster,* for the word *dictionary* is understood immediately after. Webster and Worcester do not together possess the same dictionary. The sign should not be added to *Ticknor,* for the two men, Tieknor and Field, possess the same store.

Adam's and Eve's garden; Jacob's and Esau's father; Shakespeare and Milton's works; Maud, Kate, and Clara's gloves; Maud's, Kate's, and Clara's teacher was ———.

When one possessive noun is explanatory of another, the possessive sign is added to the last only.

CORRECT THE FOLLOWING ERRORS.

I called at Tom's the tinker's.
They listened to Peter's the Hermit's eloquence.

This was the Apostle's Paul's advice.

CORRECT THE FOLLOWING ERRORS.

Our's, your's, hi's, their's, her's, it's, hisn, yourn, hern.

FORMS OF THE PRONOUN.

+Remember+ that *I, we, thou, ye, he, she, they,* and *who* are +*nominative*+ forms, and must not be used in the objective case.

+Remember+ that *me, us, thee, him, her, them,* and *whom* are +*objective*+ forms, and must not be used in the nominative case.

+To the Teacher+.—The *eight* nominative forms and the *seven* objective forms given above are the only distinctive nominative and objective forms in the English language. Let the pupils become familiar with them.

CORRECT THE FOLLOWING ERRORS.

Him and me are good friends.
The two persons were her and me.
Us girls had a jolly time.
It is them, surely.
Who will catch this? Me.
Them that despise me shall be lightly esteemed.
Who is there? Me.
It was not us, it was him.
Who did you see?
Who did you ask for?

+Remember+ that pronouns must agree with their antecedents in number, gender, and person.

CORRECT THE FOLLOWING ERRORS.

Every boy must read their own sentences.
I gave the horse oats, but he would not eat it.
Every one must read it for themselves.
I took up the little boy, and set it on my knee.

+Remember+ that the relative *who* represents persons; *which*, animals and things; *that*, persons, animals, and things; and *what*, things.

CORRECT THE FOLLOWING ERRORS.

I have a dog who runs to meet me.
The boy which I met was quite lame.
Those which live in glass houses must not throw stones.

REVIEW QUESTIONS.

+To the Teacher+.—For "Schemes," see p. 186.

How many modifications have nouns and pronouns? Name and define each. How many persons are there? Define each. How many cases are there? Define each. How do you determine the case of an explanatory noun or pronoun? What is declension? How are the forms *mine, yours*, etc., now used? What is the rule for forming the possessive case? What words are used only in the nominative case? What words are used only in the objective case? [Footnote: *Her* is used in the possessive case also.] How do you determine the number, gender, and person of pronouns?

NOUNS AND PRONOUNS—PARSING.

+To the Teacher+.—For general "Scheme" for parsing, see p. 189.

Select and parse all the nouns and pronouns in Lesson 53.

+Model for Written Parsing+.—*Elizabeth's favorite, Raleigh, was beheaded by James I.*

Elizabeth's
CLASSIFICATION. *Nouns.*
  Kind. Prop.
MODIFICATIONS. *Person*. 3d
  Number. Sing.
  Gender. Fem.
  Case. Pos.
SYNTAX. Pos. Mod. of *favorite*.

favorite
CLASSIFICATION. *Nouns.*
  Kind. Com.
MODIFICATIONS. *Person*. 3d
  Number. Sing.
  Gender. Mas.

        Case. Nom.
SYNTAX. Sub. of *was beheaded*.

 Raleigh
CLASSIFICATION. *Nouns*.
        Kind. Prop.
MODIFICATIONS. *Person*. 3d
        Number. Sing.
        Gender. Mas.
        Case. Nom.
SYNTAX. Exp. Mod. of *favorite*.

 James I.
CLASSIFICATION. *Nouns*.
        Kind. Prop.
MODIFICATIONS. *Person*. 3d
        Number. Sing.
        Gender. Mas.
        Case. Obj.
SYNTAX. Prin. word after *by*.

+To the Teacher+.—Select other exercises, and continue this work as long as it may be profitable. See Lessons 56, 57, 61, 64, and 65.

COMPARISON OF ADJECTIVES.

+Adjectives have one modification;+ viz., *Comparison*.

DEFINITIONS.

+*Comparison* is a modification of the adjective to express the relative degree of the quality in the things compared+.

+The *Positive degree* expresses the simple quality+.

+The *Comparative degree* expresses a greater or a less degree of the quality+.

+The *Superlative degree* expresses the greatest or the least degree of the quality+.

+RULE.—Adjectives are regularly compared by adding *er* to the positive to form the comparative, and *est* to the positive to form the superlative+.

Adjectives of one syllable are *generally* compared regularly; adjectives of two or more syllables are often compared by prefixing *more* and *most*.

When there are two correct forms, choose the one that can be more easily pronounced.

Compare the following adjectives. For the spelling, consult your dictionaries.

Model.—*Positive. Comparative. Superlative.*
Lovely, lovelier, loveliest; *or*
lovely, more lovely, most lovely.

Tame, warm, beautiful, brilliant, amiable, high, mad, greedy, pretty, hot.

Some adjectives are compared *irregularly*. Learn the following forms.

Positive. Comparative. Superlative.
Good, better, best.
Bad, |
Evil, + worse, worst.
Ill, |
Little, less, least.
Much, |
Many, | more, most.

COMPARISON OF ADJECTIVES AND ADVERBS.

+*Remember*+ that, when two things or groups of things are compared, the *comparative* degree is commonly used; when more than two, the *superlative* is employed.

+*Caution*+.—Adjectives should not be *doubly* compared.

CORRECT THE FOLLOWING ERRORS.

Of all the boys, George is the more industrious.
Peter was older than the twelve apostles.
Which is the longer of the rivers of America?
This was the most unkindest cut of all.
He chose a more humbler part.
My hat is more handsomer than yours.
The younger of those three boys is the smarter.
Which is the more northerly, Maine, Oregon, or Minnesota?

+*Caution*+.—Do not use adjectives and adverbs extravagantly.

CORRECT THE FOLLOWING ERRORS.

The weather is horrid.
That dress is perfectly awful.
Your coat sits frightfully.
We had an awfully good time.
This is a tremendously hard lesson.
Harry is a mighty nice boy.

+Remember+ that adjectives whose meaning does not admit of different degrees cannot be compared; as, *every, universal*.

Use in the three different degrees such of the following adjectives as admit of comparison.

All, serene, excellent, immortal, first, two, total, infinite, three-legged, bright.

+Adverbs+ are compared in the same manner as adjectives. The following are compared regularly. Compare them.

Fast, often, soon, late, early.

In the preceding and in the following list, find words that may be used as adjectives.

The following are compared irregularly. Learn them.

Pos. Comp. Sup.
_____-_____ _____

Badly, Ill, worse, worst.
Well, better, best.
Little, less, least.
Much, more, most.
Far, farther, farthest.

Adverbs ending in *ly* are generally compared by prefixing *more* and *most*. Compare the following.

Firmly, gracefully, actively, easily.

+To the Teacher+.—Let the pupils select and parse all the adjectives and adverbs in Lesson 27. For forms, see p. 189. Select other exercises, and continue the work as long as it is profitable. See "Schemes" for review, p. 188.

REVIEW QUESTIONS.

How is a noun parsed? What modification have adjectives? What is comparison? How many degrees of comparison are there? Define each. How are adjectives regularly compared? Distinguish the uses of the comparative and the superlative degree. Give the directions for using adjectives and adverbs (Lesson 88). Illustrate. What adjectives cannot be compared? How are adverbs compared?

MODIFICATION OF VERBS.

VOICE.

+Hints for Oral Instruction+.—*I picked the rose.* I will tell the same thing in another way. *The rose was picked by me.* The first verb *picked* shows that the subject *I* represents the actor, and the second form of the verb, *was picked*, shows that the subject names the thing acted upon. This change in the form of the verb is called +Voice+. The first form is called the +Active Voice+; and the second, the +Passive Voice+.

The *passive* form is very convenient when we wish to assert an action without naming any actor. *Money is coined* is better than *somebody coins money*.

DEFINITIONS.

+*Voice* is that modification of the transitive verb which shows whether the subject names the *actor* or the *thing acted upon*+.

+The *Active Voice* shows that the subject names the actor+.

+The *Passive Voice* shows that the subject names the thing acted upon+.

MODE, TENSE, NUMBER, AND PERSON.

+Hints for Oral Instruction+.—When I say, *James walks*, I assert the walking as a *fact*. When I say, *James may walk*, I do not assert the action as a fact, but as a *possible* action. When I say, *If James walk out, he will improve*, I assert the action, not as an actual fact, but as a *condition* of James's, improving. When I say to James, *Walk out*, I do not assert that James actually does the act, I assert the action as a *command*.

The action expressed by the verb *walk* has been asserted in *four* different *ways*, or +modes+. The first way is called the +Indicative Mode+; the second, the +Potential Mode+; the third, the +Subjunctive Mode+; the fourth, the +Imperative Mode+.

Let the teacher give other examples and require the pupils to repeat this instruction.

For the two forms of the verb called the +Infinitive+ and the +Participle+, see "Hints," Lessons 48 and 49.

I walk. I walked. I shall walk. In each of these three sentences, the manner of asserting the action is the same. *I walk* expresses the action as *present*. *I walked* expresses the action as *past*, and *I shall walk* expresses the action as *future*. As +Tense+ means *time*, the first form is called the

CONJUGATION OF THE VERB.

+DEFINITIONS+.

+*Conjugation* is the regular arrangement of all the forms of the verb+.

+*Synopsis* is the regular arrangement of the forms of one number and person in all the modes and tenses+.

+*Auxiliary Verbs* are those that help in the conjugation of other verbs+.

The auxiliaries are *do, be, have, shall, will, may, can,* and *must.*

+The *Principal Parts* of a verb are the present indicative or the present infinitive, the past indicative, and the past participle+.

These are called *principal parts,* because all the other forms of the verb are derived from them.

We give, below, the *principal parts* of some of the most important *irregular verbs*. Learn them.

Present. Past. Past. Par.
Be *or* am, was, been.
Begin, began, begun.

CONJUGATION OF THE VERB +SEE+ IN THE SIMPLE FORM.

+PRINCIPAL PARTS+.

Pres. Past. Past Par. See, saw, seen.

INDICATIVE MODE. PRESENT TENSE.

Singular. Plural. 1. I see, 1. We see, 2. You see, *or* 2. You see, Thou seest, 3. He sees; 3. They see.

PAST TENSE.

1. I saw, 1. We saw, 2. You saw, *or* 2. You saw, Thou sawest, 3. He saw; 3. They saw.

FUTURE TENSE.

1. I shall see, 1. We shall see, 2. You will see, *or* 2. You will see, Thou wilt see, 3. He will see; 3. They will see.

PRESENT PERFECT TENSE.

1. I have seen, 1. We have seen, 2. You have seen, *or* 2. You have seen, Thou hast seen 3. He has seen; 3. They have seen.

CONJUGATION OF THE VERB—SIMPLE FORM.

Fill out the following forms, using the principal parts of the verb *walk*. *Pres., walk; Past, walked; Past Par., walked.*

INDICATIVE MODE.

PRESENT TENSE.

Singular. Plural. 1. I / *Pres* /, 1. We / *Pres* /, 2. You / *Pres* /, 2. You / *Pres* /, Thou / *Pres* /est, 3. He / *Pres* /s; 3. They / *Pres* /.

PAST TENSE

1. I / *Past* /, 1. We / *Past* /, 2. You / *Past* /, 2. You / *Past* /, Thou / *Past* /st, 3. He / *Past* /; 3. They / *Past* /.

FUTURE TENSE.

1. I *shall* / *Pres* /, 1. We *will* / *Pres* /, 2. You *will* / *Pres* /, 2. You *will* / *Pres* /, Thou *wil-t* / *Pres* /, 3. He *will* / *Pres* /; 3. They *will* / *Pres* /.

PRESENT PERFECT TENSE.

1. I *have* /*Past Par.*/, 1. We *have* /*Past Par.*/, 2. You *have* /*Past Par.*/, 2. You *have* /*Past Par.*/, Thou *ha-st* /*Past Par.*/, 3. He *ha-s* /*Past Par.*/; 3. They

have /Past Par./.

PAST PERFECT TENSE.

1. I *had* /Past Par./, 1. We *had* /Past Par./, 2. You *had* /Past Par./, 2. You *had* /Past Par./, Thou *had-st* /Past Par./, 3. He *had* /Past Par./; 3. They *had* /Past Par./.

FUTURE PERFECT TENSE.

1. I *shall have* /Past Par./, 1. We *will have* Past Par., 2. You *will have* /Past Par./, 2. You *will have* Past Par., Thou *wil-t have* /Past Par./, 3. He *will have* /Past Par./; 3. They *will have* Past Par..

POTENTIAL MODE.

PRESENT TENSE.

1. I *may* / Pres. /, 1. We *may* / Pres. /, 2. You *may* / Pres. /, 2. You *may* / Pres. /, Thou *may-st* / Pres. /, 3. He *may* / Pres. /; 3. They *may* / Pres. /.

PAST TENSE.

1. I *might* / Pres. /, 1. We *might* / Pres. /, 2. You *might* / Pres. /, 2. You *might* / Pres. /, Thou *might-st* / Pres. /, 3. He *might* / Pres. /; 3. They *might* / Pres. /.

PRESENT PERFECT TENSE.

1. I *may have* /Past Par./, 1. We *may have* /Past Par./, 2. You *may have* /Past Par./, 2. You *may have* /Past Par./, Thou *may-st have* /Past Par./, 3. He *may have* /Past Par./; 3. They *may have* /Past Par./.

PAST PERFECT TENSE.

1. I *might have* /Past Par./, 1. We *might have* /Past Par./, 2. You *might have* /Past Par./, 2. You *might have* /Past Par./, Thou *might-st have* /Past Par./, 3. He *might have* /Past Par./; 3. They *might have* /Past Par./.

SUBJUNCTIVE MODE.

PRESENT TENSE.

Singular. Plural. 1. If I / *Pres.* /, 1. If we / *Pres.* /, 2. If you / *Pres.* /, 2. If you / *Pres.* /, If thou / *Pres.* /, 3. If he / *Pres.* /; 3. If they / *Pres.* /.

IMPERATIVE MODE.

PRESENT TENSE.

2. / *Pres.* / (you *or* thou); 2. / *Pres.* / (you).

INFINITIVES.

PRESENT TENSE.

To / *Pres.* /.

PRESENT PERFECT TENSE.

To *have* /Past Par./.

PARTICIPLES.

PRESENT. PAST. PAST PERFECT. /*Pres.*/ing. /Past Par./ Having /Past Par./

+To the Teacher+.—Let the pupils fill out these forms with other verbs. In the indicative, present, third, singular, *es* is sometimes added instead of *s*; and in the second person, old style, *st* is sometimes added instead of *est*.

CONJUGATION OF THE VERB BE.

In studying this Lesson, pay no attention to the line at the right of each verb.

INDICATIVE MODE.

PRESENT TENSE.

Singular. Plural. 1. I am ——, 1. We are ——, 2. You are —— or 2. You are ——, Thou art ——, 3. He is ——; 3. They are ——.

PAST TENSE.

1. I was ——, 1. We were ——, 2. You were ——, or 2. You were ——, Thou wast ——, 3. He was ——; 3. They were ——.

FUTURE TENSE.

1. I shall be ——, 1. We shall be ——, 2. You will be ——, or 2. You will be ——, Thou wilt be ——, 3. He will be ——; 3. They will be ——.

PRESENT PERFECT TENSE.

1. I have been ——, 1. We have been ——, 2. You have been —— or 2. You have been ——, Thou hast been ——, 3. He has been ——; 3. They

have been ———.

PAST PERFECT TENSE.

1. I had been ———, 1. We had been ———, 2. You had been ——— *or* 2. You had been ———, Thou hadst been ———, 3. He had been ———; 3. They had been ———.

FUTURE PERFECT TENSE.

1. I shall have been ———, 1. We shall have been ———, 2. You will have been ——— *or* 2. You will have been ———, Thou wilt have been ———, 3. He will has been ———; 3. They will have been ———.

POTENTIAL MODE.

PRESENT TENSE.

Singular. Plural. 1. I may be ———, 1. We may be ———, 2. You may be ——— *or* 2. You may be ———, Thou mayst be ———, 3. He may be ———; 3. They may be ———.

PAST TENSE.

1. I might be ———, 1. We might be ———, 2. You might be ——— *or* 2. You might be ———, Thou mightst be ———, 3. He might be ———; 3. They might be ———.

PRESENT PERFECT TENSE.

1. I may have been ———, 1. We may have been ———, 2. You may have been ——— *or* 2. You may have been ———, Thou mayst have been ———, 3. He may have been ———; 3. They may have been ———.

PAST PERFECT TENSE.

1. I might have been ――, 1. We might have been ――, 2. You might have been ―― *or* 2. You might have been ――, Thou mightst have been ――, 3. He might have been ――; 3. They might have been ――.

SUBJUNCTIVE MODE.

PRESENT TENSE.

Singular. Plural. 1. If I be ――, 1. If we be ――, 2. If you be ―― *or* 2. If you be ――, If thou be ――, 3. If he be ――; 3. If they be ――.

PAST TENSE.

1. If I were ――, 1. If we were ――, 2. If you were ―― *or* 2. If you were ――, If thou wert ――, 3. If he were ――; 3. If they were ――.

IMPERATIVE MODE.

PRESENT TENSE.

2. Be (you *or* them) ――; 2. Be (you) ――.

INFINITIVES.

PRESENT TENSE.
To be ――.

PRESENT PERFECT TENSE.

To have been ――.

PARTICIPLES.

PRESENT. PAST. PAST PERFECT.
Being ———. Been. Having been ———.

+To the Teacher+.—After the pupils have become thoroughly familiar with the verb *be* as a principal verb, teach them to use it as an auxiliary in making the +Progressive Form+ and the +Passive Form+.

The *progressive form* may be made by filling all the blanks with the *present participle* of some verb.

The *passive form* may be made by filling all the blanks with the *past participle* of a *transitive* verb.

Notice that, after the past participle, no blank is left.

In the progressive form, this participle is wanting; and, in the passive form, it is the same as in the simple.

AGREEMENT OF THE VERB.

+To the Teacher+.—For additional matter, see pp. 163-167.

+*Remember*+ that the verb must agree with its subject in number and person.

Give the person and number of each of the following verbs, and write sentences in which each form shall be used correctly.

Common forms.—Does, has=ha(ve)s, is, am, are, was, were.

Old forms.—Seest, sawest, hast=ha(ve)st, wilt, mayst, mightst, art, wast.

When a verb has two or more subjects connected by *and*, it must agree with them in the plural. *A similar rule applies to the agreement of the pronoun.*

CORRECT THE FOLLOWING ERRORS.

+Model+.—Poverty and obscurity *oppresses* him who thinks that *it is oppressive.*

Wrong: the verb *oppresses* should be changed to *oppress* to agree with its two subjects, connected by *and*. The pronoun *it* should be changed to *they* to agree with its two antecedents, and the verb *is* should be changed to *are* to agree with *they*.

Industry, energy, and good sense is essential to success.
Time and tide waits for no man.
The tall sunflower and the little violet is turning its face to the sun.
The mule and the horse was harnessed together.
Every green leaf and every blade of grass seem grateful.

+Model+.—The preceding sentence is wrong. The verb *seem* is plural, and it should be singular; for, when several singular subjects are preceded by *each*, every_, or *no*, they are taken separately.

Each day and each hour bring their portion of duty.
Every book and every paper were found in their place.

When a verb has two or more singular subjects connected by *or* or *nor*, it must agree with them in the singular. *A similar rule applies to the agreement of the pronoun.*

CORRECT THE FOLLOWING ERRORS.

One or the other have made a mistake in their statement.
Neither the aster nor the dahlia are cultivated for their fragrance.
Either the president or his secretary were responsible.
Neither Ann, Jane, nor Sarah are at home.

To foretell, or to express future time simply, the auxiliary *shall* is used in the first person, and *will* in the second and third; but when a speaker determines or promises, he uses *will* in the first person and *shall* in the second and third.

CORRECT THE FOLLOWING ERRORS.

I will freeze, if I do not move about.
You shall feel better soon, I think.
She shall be fifteen years old to-morrow.
I shall find it for you, if you shall bring the book to me.
You will have it, if I can get it for you.
He will have it, if he shall take the trouble to ask for it.
He will not do it, if I can prevent him.
I will drown, nobody shall help me.
I will be obliged to you, if you shall attend to it.
We will have gone by to-morrow morning.
You shall disappoint your father, if you do not return.
I do not think I will like the change.
Next Tuesday shall be your birthday.
You shall be late, if you do not hurry.

ERRORS IN THE FORM OF THE VERB.

CORRECT THE FOLLOWING ERRORS.

+Model+.—Those things *have* not *came to-day*.

Wrong, because the past *came* is here used for the past participle *come*. The present perfect tense is formed by prefixing *have* to the *past participle*.

I done all my work before breakfast.
I come in a little late yesterday.
He has went to my desk without permission.
That stupid fellow set down on my new hat.

Set is generally transitive, and *sit* is intransitive. *Lay* is transitive, and *lie* is intransitive.

He sat the chair in the corner.
Sit that plate on the table, and let it set.
I have set in this position a long time.
That child will not lay still or set still a minute.
I laid down under the tree, and enjoyed the scenery.
Lie that stick on the table, and let it lay.
Those boys were drove out of the fort three times.

I have rode through the park.
I done what I could.
He has not spoke to-day.
The leaves have fell from the trees.
This sentence is wrote badly.
He throwed his pen down, and said that the point was broke.
He teached me grammar.
I seen him when he done it.
My hat was took off my head, and throwed out of the window.
The bird has flew into that tall tree.
I was chose leader.
I have began to do better. I begun this morning.
My breakfast was ate in a hurry.
Your dress sets well.
That foolish old hen is setting on a wooden egg.
He has tore it up and throwed it away.
William has took my knife, and I am afraid he has stole it.
This should be well shook.
I begun to sing, before I knowed what I was doing.
We drunk from a pure spring.
I thought you had forsook us.
His pencil is nearly wore up.
He come, and tell me all he knowed about it.

REVIEW QUESTIONS.

+To the Teacher+.—See "Scheme," p. 187.

How many modifications have verbs? Ans.—*Five; viz., voice, mode, tense, number, and person.* Define voice. How many voices are there? Define each. Illustrate. What is mode? How many modes are there? Define each. What is an infinitive? What is a participle? How many different kinds of participles are there? Define each. Illustrate. What is tense? How many tenses are there? Define each. Illustrate. What are the number and the person of a verb? Illustrate. What is conjugation? What is synopsis? What are auxiliaries? Name the auxiliaries. What are the principal parts of a verb? Why are they so called? How does a verb agree with its subject? When a verb has two or more subjects, how does it agree? Illustrate the uses of *shall* and *will*.

+To the Teacher+.—Select some of the preceding exercises, and require the pupils to write the parsing of all the verbs. See Lessons 34, 35, 48, 49, and 56.

+Model for Written Parsing—Verbs+.—*The Yankee, selling his farm, wanders away to seek new lands.*

CLASSIFICATION. MODIFICATIONS. SYNTAX.

Verbs. Kind. Voice. Mode. Tense. Num. Per.

*selling Pr. Par., Ir., Tr. Ac. —- —- —- —- Mod. of *Yankee.* wanders Reg., Int. —- Ind. Pres. Sing. 3d. Pred. of " *seek Inf, Ir., Tt, Ac. —- " —- —- Prin. word in phrase Mod. of *wanders*.

[Footnote *: Participles and Infinitives have no *person* or *number*.]

SENTENCE-BUILDING.

Participles sometimes partake of the nature of the noun, while they retain the nature of the verb.

Build each of the following phrases into a sentence, and explain the nature of the participle.

+Model+.—— ——*in building a snow fort*. They were engaged *in building a snow fort*. The participle *building*, like a noun, follows the preposition *in*, as the principal word in the phrase; and, like a verb, it takes the object complement *fort*.

—— by foretelling storms. —— by helping others. —— on approaching the house. —— in catching fish.

Use the following phrases as subjects.

Walking in the garden ——. His writing that letter ——. Breaking a promise ——.

Use each of the following phrases in a complex sentence. Let some of the dependent clauses be used as adjectives, and some, as adverbs.

—— in sledges. —— up the Hudson. —— down the Rhine. —— through the Alps. —— with snow and ice. —— into New York Bay. —— on the prairie. —— at Saratoga.

Build a short sentence containing all the parts of speech.

Expand the following simple sentence into twelve sentences.

Astronomy teaches the size, form, nature, and motions of the sun, moon,
and stars.

Contract the following awkward compound sentence into a neat simple sentence,

Hannibal passed through Gaul, and then he crossed the Alps, and then came
down into Italy, and then he defeated several Roman generals.

Change the following complex sentences to compound sentences.

When he asked me the question, I answered him courteously.
Morse, the man who invented the telegraph, was a public benefactor.
When spring comes, the birds will return.

Contract the following complex sentences into simple sentences by changing the verb in the dependent clause to a participle. Notice all the other changes.

A ship which was gliding along the horizon attracted our attention.
I saw a man who was plowing a field.
When the shower had passed, we went on our way.
I heard that he wrote that article.

That he was a foreigner was well known.
I am not sure that he did it.
Every pupil who has an interest in this work will prepare for it.

Change the following compound sentences to complex sentences.

+Model+.—Morning dawns, and the clouds disperse. When morning dawns, the clouds disperse.

Avoid swearing; it is a wicked habit.
Pearls are valuable, and they are found in oyster shells.
Dickens wrote David Copperfield, and he died in 1870.
Some animals are vertebrates, and they have a backbone.

Expand each of the following sentences as much as you can.

Indians dance. The clock struck. The world moves.

MISCELLANEOUS ERRORS.

CORRECT THE FOLLOWING ERRORS.

I have got that book at home.

+Model+.—Wrong, because *have*, alone, asserts possession. *Got,* used in the sense of *obtained,* is correct; as, *I have just got the book.*

Have you got time to help me?
There is many mistakes in my composition.

+Model+.—Wrong, because *is* should agree with its plural subject *mistakes*. The adverb *there* is often used to introduce a sentence, that the subject may follow the predicate. This often makes the sentence sound smooth, and gives variety.

There goes my mother and sister.
Here comes the soldiers.
There was many friends to greet him.
It ain't there.

+Model+.—*Ain't* is a vulgar contraction. Correction—It *is not* there.

I have made up my mind that it ain't no use.
'Tain't so bad as you think.
Two years' interest were due.
Every one of his acts were criticised.
I, Henry, and you have been chosen.

+Model+.—Wrong, for politeness requires that you should mention the one spoken to, first; the one spoken of, next; and yourself, last.

He invited you and I and Mary.
Me and Jane are going to the fair.
I only want a little piece.
He is a handsome, tall man.
Did you sleep good?
How much trouble one has, don't they?
He inquired for some tinted ladies' note-paper.
You needn't ask me nothing about it, for I haven't got no time to answer.
Him that is diligent will succeed.
He found the place sooner than me.
Who was that? It was me and him.
If I was her, I would say less.
Bring me them tongs.
Us boys have a base-ball club.
Whom did you say that it was?
Who did you speak to just now?
Who did you mean, when you said that?
Where was you when I called?
There's twenty of us going.
Circumstances alters cases.
Tell them to set still.
He laid down by the fire.

She has lain her book aside.
It takes him everlastingly.
That was an elegant old rock.

ANALYSIS AND PARSING.

1. Thou shalt not take the name of the Lord thy God in vain. 2. Strike! till the last armed foe expires! 3. You wrong me, Brutus. 4. Shall we gather strength by irresolution and inaction? 5. Why stand we here idle? 6. Give me liberty, or give me death! 7. Thy mercy, O Lord, is in the heavens, and thy faithfulness reacheth unto the clouds. 8. The clouds poured out water, the skies sent out a sound, the voice of thy thunder was in the heaven. 9. The heavens declare his righteousness, and all the people see his glory. 10. The verdant lawn, the shady grove, the variegated landscape, the boundless ocean, and the starry firmament are beautiful and magnificent objects. 11. When you grind your corn, give not the flour to the devil and the bran to God. 12. That which the fool does in the end, the wise man does at the beginning. 13. Xerxes commanded the largest army that was ever brought into the field. 14. Without oxygen, fires would cease to burn, and all animals would immediately die. 15. Liquids, when acted upon by gravity, press downward, upward, and sideways. 16. Matter exists in three states— the solid state, the liquid state, and the gaseous state. 17. The blending of the seven prismatic colors produces white light. 18. Soap-bubbles, when they are exposed to light, exhibit colored rings. 19. He who yields to temptation debases himself with a debasement from which he can never arise. 20. Young eyes that last year smiled in ours Now point the rifle's

barrel; And hands then stained with fruits and flowers Bear redder stains of quarrel.

CAPITAL LETTERS AND PUNCTUATION.

+Capital Letters+.—The first word of (1) a sentence, (2) a line of poetry, (3) a direct quotation making complete sense or a direct question introduced into a sentence, and (4) phrases or clauses separately numbered or paragraphed should begin with a capital letter. Begin with a capital letter (5) proper names and words derived from them, (6) names of things personified, and (7) most abbreviations. Write in capital letters (8) the words *I* and *O*, and (9) numbers in the Roman notation. [Footnote: Small letters are preferred where numerous references to chapters, etc., are made.]

+Examples+.—1. The judicious are always a minority.

2. Honor and shame from no condition rise; Act well your part, there all the honor lies. 3. The question is, "Can law make people honest?" 4. Paintings are useful for these reasons: 1. They please; 2. They instruct. 5. The heroic Nelson destroyed the French fleet in Aboukir Bay. 6. Next, Anger rushed, his eyes on fire. 7. The Atlantic ocean beat Mrs. Partington. 8. The use of *O* and *oh* I am now to explain. 9. Napoleon II. never came to the throne.

+Period+.—Place a period after (1) a declarative or an imperative sentence, (2) an abbreviation, and (3) a number written in the Roman notation.

For examples see 1, 7, and 9 in the sentences above.

+Interrogation Point+.—Every direct interrogative sentence or clause should be followed by an interrogation point.

+Example+.—King Agrippa, believest thou the prophets?

+Exclamation Point+.—All exclamatory expressions must be followed by the exclamation point.

+Example+.—Oh! bloodiest picture in the book of time! +*Comma*+.—Set off by the comma (1) a phrase out of its natural order or not closely connected with the word it modifies; (2) an explanatory modifier that does not restrict the modified term or combine closely with it; (3) a participle used as an adjective modifier, with the words belonging to it, unless restrictive; (4) the adjective clause, when not restrictive; (5) the adverb clause, unless it closely follows and restricts the word it modifies; (6) a word or phrase independent or nearly so; (7) a direct quotation introduced into a sentence, unless *formally* introduced; (8) a noun clause used as an attribute complement; and (9) a term connected to another by or and having the same meaning. Separate by the comma (10) connected words and phrases, unless all the conjunctions are expressed; (11) independent clauses, when short and closely connected; and (12) the parts of a compound predicate and of other phrases, when long or differently modified.

+*Examples*+.—1. In the distance, icebergs look like masses of burnished metal. 2. Alexandria, the capital of Lower Egypt, is an ill-looking city. 3. Labor, diving deep into the earth, brings up long-hidden stores of coal. 4. The sun, which is the center of our system, is millions of miles from us. 5. When beggars die, there are no comets seen. 6. Gentlemen, this, then, is your verdict. 7. God said, "Let there be light." 8. Nelson's signal was, "England expects every man to do his duty." 9. Rubbers, or overshoes, are worn to keep the feet dry. 10. The sable, the seal, and the otter furnish us rich furs. 11. His dark eye flashed, his proud breast heaved, his cheek's hue came and went. 12. Flights of birds darken the air, and tempt the traveler with the promise of abundant provisions.

+*Semicolon*+.—Independent clauses (1) when slightly connected, or (2) when themselves divided by the comma, must be separated by the semicolon. Use the semicolon (3) between serial phrases or clauses having a common dependence on something that precedes or follows; and (4) before *as, viz., to wit., namely, i. e.,* and *that is,* when they introduce examples or illustrations.

+*Examples*+.—1. The furnace blazes; the anvil rings; the busy wheels whirl round. 2. As Caesar loved me, I weep for him; as he was fortunate, I rejoice at it; as he was valiant, I honor him; but, as he was ambitious, I slew him. 3. He drew a picture of the sufferings of our Saviour; his trial before Pilate; his ascent of Calvary; his crucifixion and death. 4. Gibbon writes, "I have been sorely afflicted with gout in the hand; to wit, laziness."

+*Colon*+.—Use the colon (1) between the parts of a sentence when these parts are themselves divided by the semicolon; and (2) before a quotation or an enumeration of particulars when formally introduced.

+*Examples*+.—1. Canning's features were handsome; his eye, though deeply ensconced under his eyebrows, was full of sparkle and gayety: the features of Brougham were harsh in the extreme. 2. To Lentullus and Gellius bear this message: "Their graves are measured."

+*Dash*+.—Use the dash where there is an omission (1) of letters or figures, and (2) of such words as *as, namely,* or *that is,* introducing illustrations or equivalent expressions. Use the dash (3) where the sentence breaks off abruptly, and the same thought is resumed after a slight suspension, or another takes its place; and (4) before a word or phrase repeated at intervals for emphasis. The dash may be used (5) instead of marks of parenthesis, and may (6) follow other marks, adding to their force.

+*Examples*+.—1. In M———w, v. 3-11, you may find the "beatitudes." 2. There are two things certain in this world—taxes and death. 3. I said—I know not what. 4. I never would lay down my arms—*never*— NEVER—+NEVER+. 5. Fulton started a steamboat——he called it the Clermont—on the Hudson in 1807. 6. My dear Sir,—I write this letter for information.

+*Marks of Parenthesis*+.—Marks of parenthesis may be used to enclose what has no essential connection with the rest of the sentence.

+Example+.—The noun (Lat. *nomen*, a name) is the first part of speech.

+*Apostrophe*+.—Use the apostrophe (1) to mark the omission of letters, (2) in the pluralizing of letters, figures, and characters, and (3) to distinguish the possessive from other cases.

+*Examples*+.—1. Bo't of John Jones 10 lbs. of butter. 2. What word is there one-half of which is *p's*? 3. He washed the disciples' feet.

+*Hyphen*+.—Use the hyphen (-) (1) between the parts of compound words that have not become consolidated, and (2) between syllables when a word is divided.

+*Examples*+.—1. Work-baskets are convenient. 2. Divide *basket* thus: *bas-ket*.

+*Quotation Marks*+—Use quotation marks to enclose a copied word or passage. If the quotation contains a quotation, the latter is enclosed within single marks.

+*Example*+—-The sermon closed with this sentence: "God said, 'Let there be light.'"

+*Brackets*+.—Use brackets [ ] to enclose what, in quoting another's words, you insert by way of explanation or correction.

+*Example*+.—The Psalmist says, "I prevented [anticipated] the dawning of the morning."

SENTENCES AND PARAGRAPHS.

+*To the Teacher*+.—It is very profitable to exercise pupils in combining simple statements into complex and compound sentences, and in resolving complex and compound sentences into simple statements. In combining statements, it is an excellent practice for the pupil to contract, expand, transpose, and to substitute different words. They thus learn to express the same thought in a variety of ways. Any reading-book or history will furnish good material for such practice. A few examples are given below.

+*Direction*+.—Combine in as many ways as possible each of the following groups of sentences:—

+*Example*+.—This man is to be pitied. He has no friends.

1. This man has no friends, and he is to be pitied. 2. This man is to be pitied, because he has no friends. 3. Because this man has no friends, he is to be pitied. 4. This man, who has no friends, is to be pitied. 5. This man, having no friends, is to be pitied. 6. This man, without friends, is to be pitied. 7. This friendless man deserves our pity.

1. The ostrich is unable to fly. It has not wings in proportion to its body.
2. Egypt is a fertile country. It is annually inundated by the Nile.
3. The nerves are little threads, or fibers. They extend, from the brain. They spread over the whole body.

4. John Gutenberg published a book. It was the first book known to have been printed on a printing-press. He was aided by the patronage of John Paust. He published it in 1455. He published it in the city of Mentz.

5. The human body is a machine. A watch is delicately constructed. This machine is more delicately constructed. A steam-engine is complicated. This machine is more complicated. A steam-engine is wonderful. This machine is more wonderful.

You see that short statements closely related in meaning may be improved by being combined. But young writers frequently use too many *ands* and other connectives, and make their sentences too long.

Long sentences should be broken up into short ones when the relations of the parts are not clear.

As clauses may be joined to form sentences, so sentences may be united to make *paragraphs*.

A +paragraph+ is a sentence or a group of related sentences developing one point or one division of a general subject.

The first word of a paragraph should begin a new line, and should be written a little farther to the right than the first words of other lines.

+Direction+.—Combine the following statements into sentences and paragraphs, and make of them a complete composition:—

Water is a liquid. It is composed of oxygen and hydrogen. It covers about three-fourths of the surface of the earth. It takes the form of ice. It takes the form of snow. It takes the form of vapor. The air is constantly taking up water from rivers, lakes, oceans, and from damp ground. Cool air contains moisture. Heated air contains more moisture. Heated air becomes lighter. It rises. It becomes cool. The moisture is condensed into fine particles. Clouds are formed. They float across the sky. The little particles unite and form rain-drops. They sprinkle the dry fields. At night the grass and flowers become cool. The air is not so cool. The warm air touches the grass and flowers. It is chilled. It loses a part of its moisture. Drops of dew are formed. Water has many uses. Men and animals drink it. Trees and plants drink it. They drink it by means of their leaves and roots. Water is a great purifier. It cleanses our bodies. It washes our clothes. It washes the dust from the leaves and the flowers. Water is a great worker. It floats vessels. It turns the wheels of mills. It is converted into steam. It is harnessed to mighty engines. It does the work of thousands of men and horses.

+*To the Teacher*+.—Condensed statements of facts, taken from some book not in the hands of your pupils, may be read to them, and they may be required to expand and combine these and group them into paragraphs.

LETTER-WRITING.

In writing a letter there are six things to consider—the *Heading*, the *Introduction*, the *Body of the Letter*, the *Conclusion*, the *Folding*, and the *Superscription*.

THE HEADING.

+*Parts*+.—The Heading consists of the name of the +Place+ at which the letter is written, and the +Date+. If you write from a city, give the door-number, the name of the street, the name of the city, and the name of the state. If you are at a hotel or a school, or any other well-known institution, its name may take the place of the door-number and the name of the street. If you write from a village or other country place, give your post-office address, the name of the county, and that of the state.

The Date consists of the month, the day of the month, and the year.

+How Written+.—Begin the Heading about an inch and a half from the top of the page—on the first ruled line of commercial note—and a little to the left of the middle of the page. If the Heading is very short, it may stand on one line. If it occupies more than one line, the second line should begin farther to the right than the first, and the third farther to the right than the second.

The Date stands upon a line by itself if the Heading occupies two or more lines.

The door-number, the day of month, and the year are written in figures, the rest in words. Each important word begins with a capital letter, each item is set off by the comma, and the whole closes with a period.

Direction.—Study what has been said, and write the following headings according to these models:—-

1. Hull, Mass., Nov. 1, 1860.
2. 1466 Colorado Ave.,
   Rochester, N. Y.,
   Apr. 3, 1870.
3. Newburyport, Mass.,
   June 30, 1826.
4. Starkville, Herkimer Co., N. Y.,
   Dec. 19, 1871.

1. n y rondout 11 1849 oct. 2. staten island port richmond 1877 25 january. 3. brooklyn march 1871 mansion house 29. 4. executive chamber vt february montpelier 1869 27. 5. washington franklin como nov 16 1874.

6. fifth ave may new york 460 9 1863. 7. washington d c march 1847 520 pennsylvania ave 16.

THE INTRODUCTION.

+*Parts*+.—The Introduction consists of the +*Address*+—the Name, the Title, and the Place of Business or the Residence of the one addressed—and the +*Salutation*+. Titles of respect and courtesy should appear in the Address. Prefix *Mr.* (plural, *Messrs.*) to a man's name; *Master* to a boy's name; *Miss* to the name of a girl or an unmarried lady; *Mrs.* to the name of a married lady. Prefix *Dr.* to the name of a physician, or write *M.D.* after his name. Prefix *Rev.* (or *The Rev.*) to the name of a clergyman; if he is a Doctor of Divinity, prefix *Rev. Dr.*, or write *Rev.* before his name and *D.D.* after it; if you do not know his Christian name, prefix *Rev. Mr.* or *Rev. Dr.* to his surname, but never *Rev.* alone. *Esq.* is added to the name of a lawyer, and to the names of other prominent men. Avoid such combinations as the following: *Mr. John Smith, Esq., Dr. John Smith, M.D., Mr. John Smith, M.D.*, etc.

Salutations vary with the station of the one addressed, or the writer's degree of intimacy with him. Strangers may be addressed as *Sir, Rev. Sir, General, Madam, Miss Brown,* etc.; acquaintances as *Dear Sir, Dear Madam,* etc.; friends as *My dear Sir, My dear Madam, My dear Mr. Brown,* etc.; and near relatives and other dear friends as *My dear Wife, My dear Boy, Dearest Ellen,* etc.

+*How Written*+.—The Address may follow the Heading, beginning on the next line, or the next but one, and standing on the left side of the page; or it may stand in corresponding position after the Body of the Letter and the Conclusion. If the letter is written to a very intimate friend, the Address may appropriately be placed at the bottom of the letter; but in other letters, especially those on ordinary business, it should be placed at the top and as directed above. There should always be a narrow margin on the left-hand side of the page, and the Address should always begin on the marginal line. If the Address occupies more than one line, the initial words of these lines should slope to the right, as in the Heading.

Begin the Salutation on the marginal line or a little to the right of it, when the Address occupies three lines; on the marginal line or farther to the right than the second line of the Address begins, when this occupies two lines; a little to the right of the marginal lime, when the Address occupies one line; on the marginal line, when the Address stands below.

Every important word in the Address should begin with a capital letter. All the items of it should be set off by the comma, and, as it is an abbreviated sentence, it should close with a period. Every important word in the Salutation should begin with a capital letter, and the whole should be followed by a comma.

+Direction+.—Study what has been said, and write the following introductions according to these models:—

1. Dear Father,
     I write, etc.

2. The Rev. M. H. Buckham, D.D.,
   President of U. V. M.,
     Burlington, Vt.
My dear Sir,

3. Messrs. Clark & Brown,
   Quogue, N. Y.
Gentlemen,

4. Messrs. Tiffany & Co.,
   2 Milk St., Boston.
Dear Sirs,

1. david h cochran lld president of polytechnic institute brooklyn my dear sir. 2. dr John h hobart burge 64 livingston st brooklyn n y sir. 3. prof geo n boardman Chicago ill dear teacher. 4. to the president executive mansion Washington d c mr president. 5. rev t k beecher elmira n y sir. 6. messrs gilbert & sons gentlemen mass boston. 7. mr george r curtis minn rochester my friend dear. 8. to the honorable wm m evarts secretary of state Washington d c sir.

THE BODY OF THE LETTER.

+*The Beginning*+.—Begin the Body of the Letter at the end of the Salutation, and on the *same* line, if the Introduction consists of four lines—in which case the comma after the Salutation should be followed by a dash;—otherwise, on the line *below*.

+*Style*+.—Be perspicuous. Paragraph and punctuate as in other kinds of writing. Spell correctly; write legibly, neatly, and with care.

Letters of friendship should be colloquial, natural, and familiar. Whatever is interesting to you will be interesting to your friends.

Business letters should be brief, and the sentences should be short, concise, and to the point.

In *formal notes* the third person is generally used instead of the first and the second; there is no Introduction, no Conclusion, no Signature, only the name of the Place and the Date at the bottom, on the left side of the page.

THE CONCLUSION.

+*Parts*+.—The Conclusion consists of the +*Complimentary Close*+ and the +*Signature*+. The forms of the Complimentary Close are many, and are determined by the relations of the writer to the one addressed. In letters of *friendship* you may use *Your sincere friend; Yours affectionately ; Your loving son or daughter*, etc. In business letters, you may use *Yours; Yours truly; Truly yours; Yours respectfully; Very respectfully yours*, etc. In official letters use *I have the honor to be, Sir, your obedient servant; Very respectfully, your most obedient servant.*

The Signature consists of your Christian name and your surname. In addressing a stranger write your Christian name in full. A lady addressing a stranger should prefix her title—*Miss* or *Mrs.*—to her own name, enclosing it within marks of parenthesis, if she prefers.

+*How Written*+.—The Conclusion should begin near the middle of the first line below the Body of the Letter, and should slope to the right like the Heading and the Address. Begin each line of it with a capital letter, and punctuate as in other writing, following the whole with a period. The Signature should be very plain.

THE FOLDING.

The Folding is a simple matter when, as now, the envelope used is adapted in length to the width of the sheet. Take the letter as it lies before you, with its first page uppermost, turn up the bottom of it about one-third the length of the sheet, bring the top down over this, taking care that the sides are even, and press the parts together.

Taking the envelope with its back toward you, insert the letter, putting in first the edge last folded. The form of the envelope may require the letter to be folded in the middle. Other conditions may require other ways of folding.

www.ingramcontent.com/pod-product-compliance
Lightning Source LLC
Chambersburg PA
CBHW081730100526
44591CB00016B/2567